VIOLA

101 CHRISTMAS SONGS

Available for
FLUTE, CLARINET, ALTO SAX, TENOR SAX, TRUMPET,
HORN, TROMBONE, VIOLIN, VIOLA, CELLO

ISBN 978-1-5400-3028-3

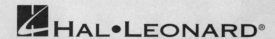

Visit Hal Leonard Online at
www.halleonard.com

Contact Us:
Hal Leonard
7777 West Bluemound Road
Milwaukee, WI 53213
Email: info@halleonard.com

In Europe contact:
Hal Leonard Europe Limited
42 Wigmore Street
Marylebone, London, W1U 2RN
Email: info@halleonardeurope.com

In Australia contact:
Hal Leonard Australia Pty. Ltd.
4 Lentara Court
Cheltenham, Victoria, 3192 Australia
Email: info@halleonard.com.au

CONTENTS

ALL I WANT FOR CHRISTMAS IS YOU

VIOLA

Words and Music by MARIAH CAREY
and WALTER AFANASIEFF

ANGELS FROM THE REALMS OF GLORY

Words by JAMES MONTGOMERY
Music by HENRY T. SMART

AS LONG AS THERE'S CHRISTMAS

from BEAUTY AND THE BEAST - THE ENCHANTED CHRISTMAS

VIOLA

Music by RACHEL PORTMAN
Lyrics by DON BLACK

Moderately

AULD LANG SYNE

VIOLA

Words by ROBERT BURNS
Traditional Scottish Melody

Moderately

ANGELS WE HAVE HEARD ON HIGH

Traditional French Carol

Moderately

AWAY IN A MANGER

Music by JAMES R. MURRAY

BABY, IT'S COLD OUTSIDE

VIOLA

By FRANK LOESSER

Moderately

AWAY IN A MANGER

VIOLA

Music by JONATHAN E. SPILMAN

Sweetly

BECAUSE IT'S CHRISTMAS
(For All the Children)

Music by BARRY MANILOW
Lyric by BRUCE SUSSMAN and JACK FELDMAN

Moderately slow

BELIEVE
from Warner Bros. Pictures' THE POLAR EXPRESS

VIOLA

Words and Music by GLEN BALLARD
and ALAN SILVESTRI

Moderately slow

BLUE CHRISTMAS

Words and Music by BILLY HAYES
and JAY JOHNSON

With expression

BRAZILIAN SLEIGH BELLS

VIOLA

By PERCY FAITH

Bright Samba

To Coda

VIOLA

CAROLING, CAROLING

Words by WIHLA HUTSON
Music by ALFRED BURT

With a lilt

THE BELLS OF ST. MARY'S

VIOLA

Traditional
Words by DOUGLAS FURBER
Music by A. EMMETT ADAMS

Slowly, with freedom

A CHILD IS BORN

VIOLA

By THAD JONES

Slowly

THE CHIPMUNK SONG

Words and Music by
ROSS BAGDASARIAN

Happily

CHRISTMAS IN KILLARNEY

Words and Music by JOHN REDMOND
and FRANK WELDON

Moderately, with a lilt

CHRISTMAS
(Baby Please Come Home)

VIOLA

Words and Music by PHIL SPECTOR,
ELLIE GREENWICH and JEFF BARRY

CHRISTMAS IS A-COMIN'
(May God Bless You)

VIOLA

Words and Music by
FRANK LUTHER

Moderately slow

Very slowly

THE CHRISTMAS SONG
(Chestnuts Roasting on an Open Fire)

VIOLA

Music and Lyric by MEL TORMÉ
and ROBERT WELLS

DO YOU WANT TO BUILD A SNOWMAN?

from FROZEN

VIOLA

Music and Lyrics by KRISTEN ANDERSON-LOPEZ
and ROBERT LOPEZ

COLD DECEMBER NIGHT

VIOLA

Words and Music by MICHAEL BUBLE,
ALAN CHANG and ROBERT ROCK

CHRISTMAS TIME IS HERE
from A CHARLIE BROWN CHRISTMAS

VIOLA

Words by LEE MENDELSON
Music by VINCE GUARALDI

Slowly

THE CHRISTMAS WALTZ

Words by SAMMY CAHN
Music by JULE STYNE

Moderately, with expression

DANCE OF THE SUGAR PLUM FAIRY
from THE NUTCRACKER

By PYOTR IL'YICH TCHAIKOVSKY

Quickly

DECK THE HALL

VIOLA

Traditional Welsh Carol

Brightly

DO YOU HEAR WHAT I HEAR

Words and Music by NOEL REGNEY
and GLORIA SHAYNE

Moderately

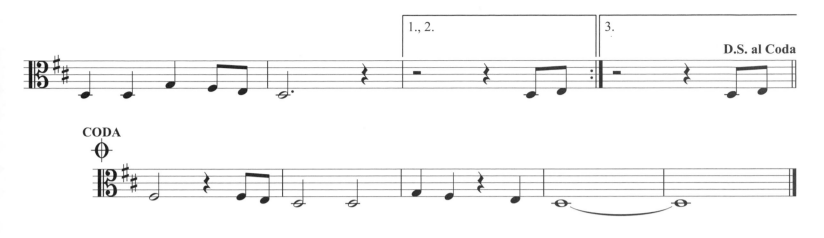

THE FIRST NOEL

17th Century English Carol
Music from W. Sandys' *Christmas Carols*

Moderately slow

FAIRYTALE OF NEW YORK

VIOLA

Words and Music by JEREMY FINER
and SHANE MacGOWAN

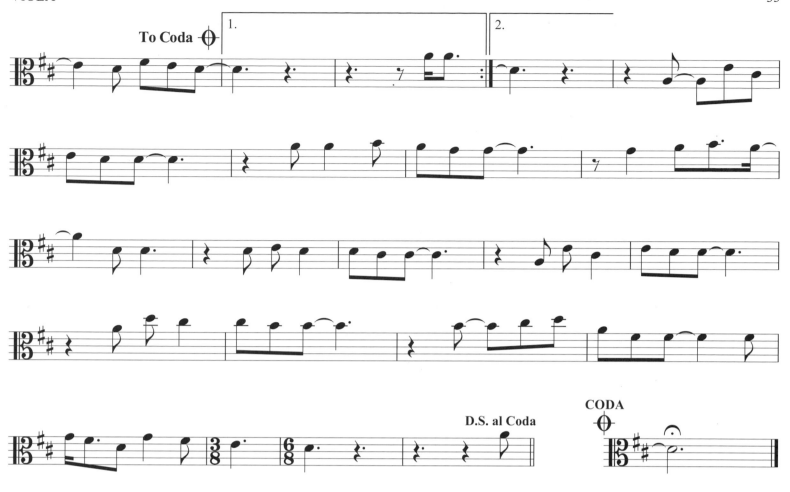

GOD REST YE MERRY, GENTLEMEN

Traditional English Carol

FELIZ NAVIDAD

VIOLA

Music and Lyrics by
JOSÉ FELICIANO

GRANDMA GOT RUN OVER BY A REINDEER

VIOLA

Words and Music by
RANDY BROOKS

THE GREATEST GIFT OF ALL

VIOLA

Words and Music by
JOHN JARVIS

Moderately slow

GOOD KING WENCESLAS

Words by JOHN M. NEALE
Music from *Piae Cantiones*

Moderately

GROWN-UP CHRISTMAS LIST

VIOLA

Words and Music by DAVID FOSTER
and LINDA THOMPSON-JENNER

Moderately slow

HARK! THE HERALD ANGELS SING

Words by CHARLES WESLEY
Music by FELIX MENDELSSOHN-BARTHOLDY

Moderately

HAPPY XMAS
(War Is Over)

VIOLA

Written by JOHN LENNON
and YOKO ONO

HAVE YOURSELF A MERRY LITTLE CHRISTMAS

from MEET ME IN ST. LOUIS

VIOLA

Words and Music by HUGH MARTIN
and RALPH BLANE

Moderately slow

HAPPY HOLIDAY
from the Motion Picture Irving Berlin's HOLIDAY INN

VIOLA

Words and Music by
IRVING BERLIN

Slowly

HARD CANDY CHRISTMAS
from THE BEST LITTLE WHOREHOUSE IN TEXAS

Words and Music by
CAROL HALL

Moderately

HERE COMES SANTA CLAUS
(Right Down Santa Claus Lane)

Words and Music by GENE AUTRY
and OAKLEY HALDEMAN

(There's No Place Like)
HOME FOR THE HOLIDAYS

VIOLA

Words and Music by AL STILLMAN
and ROBERT ALLEN

Moderately

I HEARD THE BELLS ON CHRISTMAS DAY

VIOLA

Words by HENRY WADSWORTH LONGFELLOW
Music by JOHN BAPTISTE CALKIN

Moderately slow

A HOLLY JOLLY CHRISTMAS

Music and Lyrics by
JOHNNY MARKS

Moderately bright

I WANT A HIPPOPOTAMUS FOR CHRISTMAS
(Hippo the Hero)

VIOLA

Words and Music by
JOHN ROX

I'LL BE HOME FOR CHRISTMAS

Words and Music by KIM GANNON
and WALTER KENT

Slowly

I HEARD THE BELLS ON CHRISTMAS DAY

VIOLA

Words by HENRY WADSWORTH LONGFELLOW
Adapted by JOHNNY MARKS
Music by JOHNNY MARKS

Moderately

I SAW MOMMY KISSING SANTA CLAUS

Words and Music by
TOMMIE CONNOR

Moderately slow

I SAW THREE SHIPS

VIOLA

Traditional English Carol

Brightly

I WONDER AS I WANDER

By JOHN JACOB NILES

Slowly

I'VE GOT MY LOVE TO KEEP ME WARM

from the 20th Century Fox Motion Picture ON THE AVENUE

VIOLA

Words and Music by
IRVING BERLIN

Bright Jump tempo

IT'S BEGINNING TO LOOK LIKE CHRISTMAS

VIOLA

By MEREDITH WILLSON

IT MUST HAVE BEEN THE MISTLETOE
(Our First Christmas)

VIOLA

By JUSTIN WILDE
and DOUG KONECKY

Moderately

IT CAME UPON THE MIDNIGHT CLEAR

Words by EDMUND H. SEARS
Traditional English Melody
Adapted by ARTHUR SULLIVAN

Moderately

JINGLE BELLS

VIOLA

Words and Music by
J. PIERPONT

THE LAST MONTH OF THE YEAR
(What Month Was Jesus Born In?)

Words and Music by VERA HALL
Adapted and Arranged by RUBY PICKENS TARTT
and ALAN LOMAX

LET IT SNOW! LET IT SNOW! LET IT SNOW!

Words by SAMMY CAHN
Music by JULE STYNE

JOY TO THE WORLD

VIOLA

Words by ISAAC WATTS
Music by GEORGE FRIDERIC HANDEL

Brightly

MARY'S LITTLE BOY CHILD

Words and Music by
JESTER HAIRSTON

Slowly and simply

LITTLE SAINT NICK

VIOLA

Words and Music by BRIAN WILSON
and MIKE LOVE

MARCH OF THE TOYS

from BABES IN TOYLAND

VIOLA

By VICTOR HERBERT

With spirit

A MARSHMALLOW WORLD

VIOLA

Words by CARL SIGMAN
Music by PETER DE ROSE

With motion

MARY, DID YOU KNOW?

VIOLA

Words and Music by MARK LOWRY
and BUDDY GREENE

MERRY CHRISTMAS, DARLING

VIOLA

Words and Music by RICHARD CARPENTER
and FRANK POOLER

Freely

THE MOST WONDERFUL TIME OF THE YEAR

VIOLA

Words and Music by EDDIE POLA
and GEORGE WYLE

MY FAVORITE THINGS

from THE SOUND OF MUSIC

VIOLA

Lyrics by OSCAR HAMMERSTEIN II
Music by RICHARD RODGERS

MELE KALIKIMAKA

VIOLA

Words and Music by
R. ALEX ANDERSON

MISTER SANTA

Words and Music by
PAT BALLARD

MISTLETOE AND HOLLY

Words and Music by FRANK SINATRA,
DOK STANFORD and HENRY W. SANICOLA

O LITTLE TOWN OF BETHLEHEM

VIOLA

Words by PHILLIPS BROOKS
Music by LEWIS H. REDNER

Slowly

O HOLY NIGHT

French words by PLACIDE CAPPEAU
English words by JOHN S. DWIGHT
Music by ADOLPHE ADAM

Moderately

SANTA CLAUS IS COMIN' TO TOWN

Words by HAVEN GILLESPIE
Music by J. FRED COOTS

O CHRISTMAS TREE

VIOLA

Traditional German Carol

O COME, ALL YE FAITHFUL

Music by JOHN FRANCIS WADE

PARADE OF THE WOODEN SOLDIERS

VIOLA

English Lyrics by BALLARD MacDONALD
Music by LEON JESSEL

PRETTY PAPER

VIOLA

Words and Music by
WILLIE NELSON

Flowing

ROCKIN' AROUND THE CHRISTMAS TREE

VIOLA

Music and Lyrics by
JOHNNY MARKS

Moderate Rock

RUDOLPH THE RED-NOSED REINDEER

VIOLA

Music and Lyrics by
JOHNNY MARKS

SANTA BABY

VIOLA

By JOAN JAVITS,
PHIL SPRINGER and TONY SPRINGER

Moderately slow

SHAKE ME I RATTLE
(Squeeze Me I Cry)

VIOLA

Words and Music by HAL HACKADY
and CHARLES NAYLOR

Moderately slow

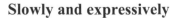

SILVER AND GOLD

Music and Lyrics by
JOHNNY MARKS

Slowly and expressively

SILVER BELLS
from the Paramount Picture THE LEMON DROP KID

Words and Music by JAY LIVINGSTON
and RAY EVANS

Moderately

THAT'S CHRISTMAS TO ME

VIOLA

Words and Music by KEVIN OLUSOLA
and SCOTT HOYING

Moderately

SILENT NIGHT

VIOLA

Words by JOSEPH MOHR
Translated by JOHN F. YOUNG
Music by FRANZ X. GRUBER

SING WE NOW OF CHRISTMAS

Traditional French Carol

SOMEWHERE IN MY MEMORY

from the Twentieth Century Fox Motion Picture HOME ALONE

VIOLA

Words by LESLIE BRICUSSE
Music by JOHN WILLIAMS

Gently and with simplicity

THE STAR CAROL

Lyric by WIHLA HUTSON
Music by ALFRED BURT

Tenderly, with much expression

THIS CHRISTMAS

VIOLA

Words and Music by DONNY HATHAWAY
and NADINE McKINNOR

TOYLAND
from BABES IN TOYLAND

VIOLA

Words by GLEN MacDONOUGH
Music by VICTOR HERBERT

Slowly

UP ON THE HOUSETOP

Words and Music by
B.R. HANBY

Brightly

WE NEED A LITTLE CHRISTMAS

from MAME

VIOLA

Music and Lyric by
JERRY HERMAN

THE TWELVE DAYS OF CHRISTMAS

VIOLA

Traditional English Carol

Moderately

Verse 1

Verses 2-4

Verse 5

Verses 6-12

These bars are played a different number of times for each verse.

WE WISH YOU THE MERRIEST

VIOLA

Words and Music by
LES BROWN

WE THREE KINGS OF ORIENT ARE

VIOLA

Words and Music by
JOHN H. HOPKINS, JR.

WE WISH YOU A MERRY CHRISTMAS

Traditional English Folksong

WHAT ARE YOU DOING NEW YEAR'S EVE?

VIOLA

By FRANK LOESSER

Slowly and sentimentally

WONDERFUL CHRISTMASTIME

VIOLA

Words and Music by
PAUL McCARTNEY

WHAT CHILD IS THIS?

VIOLA

Words by WILLIAM C. DIX
16th Century English Melody

Moderately slow

WHITE CHRISTMAS
from the Motion Picture Irving Berlin's HOLIDAY INN

Words and Music by
IRVING BERLIN

Slowly, in 2

YOU'RE ALL I WANT FOR CHRISTMAS

Words and Music by GLEN MOORE
and SEGER ELLIS

Slowly and evenly

THE WONDERFUL WORLD OF CHRISTMAS

VIOLA

Words by CHARLES TOBIAS
Music by AL FRISCH

Moderately slow

A little faster

A Tempo

101 SONGS

BIG COLLECTIONS OF FAVORITE SONGS ARRANGED FOR SOLO INSTRUMENTALISTS.

101 BROADWAY SONGS

00154199	Flute	$15.99
00154200	Clarinet	$15.99
00154201	Alto Sax	$15.99
00154202	Tenor Sax	$16.99
00154203	Trumpet	$15.99
00154204	Horn	$15.99
00154205	Trombone	$15.99
00154206	Violin	$15.99
00154207	Viola	$15.99
00154208	Cello	$15.99

101 DISNEY SONGS

00244104	Flute	$17.99
00244106	Clarinet	$17.99
00244107	Alto Sax	$17.99
00244108	Tenor Sax	$17.99
00244109	Trumpet	$17.99
00244112	Horn	$17.99
00244120	Trombone	$17.99
00244121	Violin	$17.99
00244125	Viola	$17.99
00244126	Cello	$17.99

101 MOVIE HITS

00158087	Flute	$15.99
00158088	Clarinet	$15.99
00158089	Alto Sax	$15.99
00158090	Tenor Sax	$15.99
00158091	Trumpet	$15.99
00158092	Horn	$15.99
00158093	Trombone	$15.99
00158094	Violin	$15.99
00158095	Viola	$15.99
00158096	Cello	$15.99

101 CHRISTMAS SONGS

00278637	Flute	$15.99
00278638	Clarinet	$15.99
00278639	Alto Sax	$15.99
00278640	Tenor Sax	$15.99
00278641	Trumpet	$15.99
00278642	Horn	$14.99
00278643	Trombone	$15.99
00278644	Violin	$15.99
00278645	Viola	$15.99
00278646	Cello	$15.99

101 HIT SONGS

00194561	Flute	$17.99
00197182	Clarinet	$17.99
00197183	Alto Sax	$17.99
00197184	Tenor Sax	$17.99
00197185	Trumpet	$17.99
00197186	Horn	$17.99
00197187	Trombone	$17.99
00197188	Violin	$17.99
00197189	Viola	$17.99
00197190	Cello	$17.99

101 POPULAR SONGS

00224722	Flute	$17.99
00224723	Clarinet	$17.99
00224724	Alto Sax	$17.99
00224725	Tenor Sax	$17.99
00224726	Trumpet	$17.99
00224727	Horn	$17.99
00224728	Trombone	$17.99
00224729	Violin	$17.99
00224730	Viola	$17.99
00224731	Cello	$17.99

101 CLASSICAL THEMES

00155315	Flute	$15.99
00155317	Clarinet	$15.99
00155318	Alto Sax	$15.99
00155319	Tenor Sax	$15.99
00155320	Trumpet	$15.99
00155321	Horn	$15.99
00155322	Trombone	$15.99
00155323	Violin	$15.99
00155324	Viola	$15.99
00155325	Cello	$15.99

101 JAZZ SONGS

00146363	Flute	$15.99
00146364	Clarinet	$15.99
00146366	Alto Sax	$15.99
00146367	Tenor Sax	$15.99
00146368	Trumpet	$15.99
00146369	Horn	$14.99
00146370	Trombone	$15.99
00146371	Violin	$15.99
00146372	Viola	$15.99
00146373	Cello	$15.99

101 MOST BEAUTIFUL SONGS

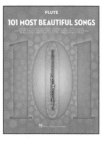

00291023	Flute	$16.99
00291041	Clarinet	$16.99
00291042	Alto Sax	$17.99
00291043	Tenor Sax	$17.99
00291044	Trumpet	$16.99
00291045	Horn	$16.99
00291046	Trombone	$16.99
00291047	Violin	$16.99
00291048	Viola	$16.99
00291049	Cello	$17.99

See complete song lists and sample pages at www.halleonard.com

HAL•LEONARD®
www.halleonard.com

Prices, contents and availability subject to change without notice.